the Kitten

A guide to selection, outfit, nutrition, care, upbringing, training and health

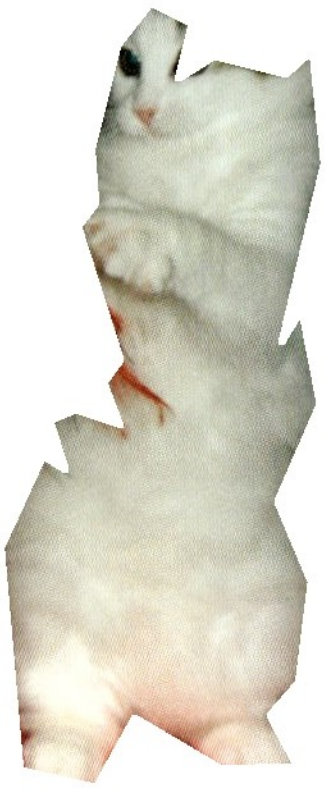

Contents

Foreword

You have probably bought this book because you're about to take a kitten into your home. That alone is reason enough to congratulate you, because that friendly ball of fur will change your life. On the one hand positively but on the other hand, certainly in the first few months, it will mean some stress.

During that period, you will lay the foundations for an intensive, and often wonderful, friendship between man and animal. Now is the moment to form your cat's character. In the first year, it will learn more than in the rest of its life and the impressions you give now will stick with it for ever. So, it's up to you to acquaint your kitten with as many situations as possible, so that you enjoy a pretty and affectionate cat.

To build up a good relationship with your kitten, a few practical matters are important. So this book pays attention to buying, feeding and caring for a kitten and its place in the home. We then discuss the various phases of a kitten's life and its upbringing.

If you know what you're doing, your pet will enjoy a better life. The basic knowledge is in this book. But when you buy a kitten, you're also taking on a responsibility to care for it properly. In return, you will be rewarded by a good deal of love and affection.

About Pets

about pets

A Publication of About Pets.

co-publisher United Kingdom
Kingdom Books
PO9 5TL, England

ISBN 1852792205
First printing
September 2003
Second printing
May 2004

Original title: *de Praktische Kattenwijzer*

Warffum, the Netherlands
http://www.aboutpets.info

Photos:
Foto's: A. Tasseron,
H. Alstede, Rob Dekker, Europet,
Dhr. van Tuijl, Isabelle Francais,
F.S. de Bruin, I. Landman, Mevr. Baaten,
M. van Haaren, Virbac, D. Kohnen, A. Hoos,
WMP and Emax

Printed in China

A kitten... what now?

The question comes up at some time in almost every family: "Should we get a kitten?" Cats are loveable, good company and like to live in the company of humans. Kittens are fun to watch too, and they have a high "cuddlability factor".

Things to think about

Never take the decision to buy a cat on impulse, even if it's love at first sight. A cat in the home is a major change for the whole family; it's another member of the family and it needs attention, daily care and can't live on air. Apart from that, turning a kitten into a friend for years costs time and energy.

There are reasons enough for a family not to get a cat. On the other hand, there are just as many reasons to do so. One thing must be certain: never buy a cat as a toy for your children to play with, but only if you want one yourself. A child can never take care of a cat alone or take responsibility for the animal. Even if all those eager promises came straight from the heart, other things will occupy a child's attention over time. You will very probably end up taking a (large) share in the care of the cat.

Once you've decided to buy a cat, you need to decide what kind of cat best fits your circumstances. A longhaired cat needs intensive, time-consuming grooming, a female will go on heat at certain times, and some breeds are heavier and livelier than others, so good thought needs to be given to the breed, sex and even the size you want your cat to be.

During your thinking, don't forget the following:

- Your kitten needs to get used to its new surroundings.
- A kitten is, by nature, a clean animal, but needs to be taught to use its

litter box. Once in a while there will be an 'accident' in the house.

- Your kitten needs periods of rest while growing. Make sure it gets these.
- With a cat in the family, you can't simply go away on holiday. It must go into kennels or you must find somebody that can care for it properly.
- A cat is not a pack animal (such as a dog), but loves company. It won't be good for it to spend long periods alone.
- Looking after your cat will cost more than just time and energy; it will cost money too. You should consider an amount between £150 and £300 per year (vet's costs, cat litter, food and other expenses).

Golden rules for a good relationship

1. Your cat will always be your best friend.
2. A cat does not have human comprehension and can't think logically. But it will remember bad experiences.
3. If man and cat spend lots of intensive time together, an emotional bond will develop.
4. Every cat is unique in terms of learning and ability to adapt and relate to humans.
5. A cat owner must discover the cat's personality, adapt to it and then form and develop it.
6. A cat will learn to adapt to humans and will closely watch human body-talk.
7. Tact and love must always predominate in the way you treat your cat.
8. A cat possesses a strong hunting instinct. It displays this every time it plays with you. Apart from this, playing together strengthens the bond between you and your cat.
9. Reward and punishment, given at just the right moment, produce the best results. Hitting a cat is way out of line. It will only have the opposite effect to what you hoped to achieve.

Where to buy your cat

This book assumes you've decided to get a kitten. The easiest place to buy one is often from a good breeder, especially if you're looking for a thoroughbred animal. But there are also other options that you should consider.

First comes the choice between a kitten, an adult cat or a somewhat older animal. Then you can choose between a female and a male, and finally you have the options of a thoroughbred cat or a normal house cat. A kitten is a playful, lively companion. You can bring it up yourself and it will easily get used to its new surroundings. Things may be different with an older cat, but there's still a lot to be said in favour of an adult animal. An older cat is quieter and will often have a 'profile' which is already known. If this fits your

circumstances and wishes, then it will become a fine companion. You can often get a normal house cat from friends or neighbours. An animal shelter is also a good alternative. There are plenty of animals there waiting for a new home, and most cats to be found there are excellent house cats. You can usually learn what you need to know about each animal from talking to the shelter's staff. All animals in shelters get first-class medical care; the staff can always tell you if there's been any disease in the shelter, and whether your cat has been vaccinated and wormed. If you choose a thoroughbred cat, get plenty of information in advance about the breed concerned. This will help you to understand your cat's character a little, and exactly how it will look later. It's a good idea to visit a cat show where you can gather lots of information and look at the breed of your choice 'in the flesh'.

Things to watch out for

So you've decided to get a kitten and, of course, you want an animal that's healthy. Unfortunately, you can't always be 100% sure that a kitten is totally healthy, but there are a few guidelines to help you be as sure as possible:

- A cat should never be shy or withdrawn. It should come to you spontaneously when you call it, and should not be frightened if you pick it up or cuddle it.
- A cat should be clean. Its coat must be springy and not show any thin or bare patches. The hair around its anus should be clean. Remains from its droppings may be a sign that it has or had diarrhoea and that is not a good sign.
- Its ears must be completely clean. Black, gritty discharge can be a sign of ear-mite infection (a parasite).
- Its eyes should not be watery.
- Its nose should be clean and dry, or a little damp. Discharge from the eyes, and especially the nose, can be a sign of cat flu or other ailments.
- A cat should have a nicely filled tummy, but it should not be round or feel sloppy. This might be an indication that the animal is suffering from peritonitis.
- Sneezing, coughing or wheezing can be signs of cat flu.
- Kittens that are too thin or too small have not been properly fed or are underdeveloped. You should be able to feel a kitten's ribs, but not see them. You should be able to feel the two points at the small of its back, but they must certainly not stick out.

Spring and autumn kittens

The view is still widespread that cats born in the autumn are weaker than those born in the spring. In principle, this need not be the case, but it does depend on where your young cat has come from. Cats that live wild and have to fend for themselves bear their young in all seasons, just like any other cat. For cats living outdoors, it's an advantage to have been born in the spring. Summer begins at about the same time as they can stand on their own feet. Most of the animals they hunt are present in plenty, the temperature has increased and the weather conditions are favourable for life and survival.

The opposite applies to so-called autumn kittens: if they're born in September, then they have to fend for themselves in terms of food from November. At the beginning they get their mother's milk, then their mother brings them animals she has killed, but at a certain moment the young have to take care of themselves. That's not a simple challenge in a cold and wet season. There is a lot less natural food available, and obviously such cats have less resistance to disease than a well-fed spring kitten. Strong or weak, it's not a good idea to try to domesticate a cat that's lived in the wild. Their kittens have often had almost no contact with humans and they will remain shy their whole lives. With kittens that are born in the home with humans around, there is no

difference between spring kittens and autumn kittens. If they're properly looked after and fed, kittens born in the autumn will also grow up healthy and strong.

Male or female

There is no reason to suggest that you should take either a male or a female cat. This decision is purely personal, but there are small differences in their care and in their behaviour. Tom-cats generally need more space than females. They have a somewhat stronger territorial instinct. Some people claim that males are more affectionate than females.

Both male and female mature both sexually and otherwise. This is first apparent in males when they go out marking their territory with their urine.

This happens at between six and eight months. Most people regard this as strange behaviour but, in fact, it is simply natural. Females don't spray, but go on heat. At what age this happens depends on the breed and living conditions, but it usually takes place between five and eleven months. A female on heat is fertile and ready to breed. She will try to 'entice' a male with typical behaviour: she will miaow loudly, often with an accompanying rasping sound, roll around on the ground and will be especially affectionate.

Both these behaviour patterns can be prevented by castration. Castration of the female is popularly known (wrongly) as spaying and neutering. In a routine operation, the vet makes both male and female infertile, and their sexual instinct no longer plays a role. The undesirable behaviour then also vanishes. In most cases, the male will cease spraying and the female will no longer go on heat.

If you do plan to breed a litter with your female, she cannot be castrated. The operation is irreversible, so in this case it's better to give her the contraceptive pill for cats. However, this is not a long-term solution because of possible side-effects. When you do decide to breed, stop giving her the pill and wait for one more season to pass before letting her mate.

One or two kittens?

A cat is not a pack animal, but does love company. If your kitten is to be alone during the day, it's better to get two kittens at the same time. The young animals will then not get bored and will keep each other busy instead of getting up to mischief. Two kittens together will do less damage than one kitten that spends all day alone in a quiet house. If you do get two kittens, try to get two females. A male and female may very quickly surprise you with offspring, if you haven't taken timely measures to prevent this. If you take two males, have them castrated in good time to prevent spraying.

The cat's outfit

Just like at the birth of a baby, a cat needs a complete outfit before it comes into the home. This is your investment in a good life for your cat.

Basket

The first basket is not a matter for too much concern. It can even be a cardboard box. With a soft blanket or cushion, your kitten will feel comfortable and at home. As it grows, you can buy a proper basket, which should stand in a quiet, warm and dry place, away from draughts, near a radiator for instance.

Food and drink bowls

Your kitten needs three bowls; one for dry food, one for canned food and one to drink from. The best bowls are those made of glazed pottery: they are the easiest to keep clean. A positive side-effect is that they can't be slid around as easily as lighter plastic dishes for example. A kitten must always have fresh drinking water available.

Your kitten's outfit

- basket with a blanket or cushion
- food and drink bowls
- litter box with cat litter
- kitten food
- travel basket
- scratching pole or plank
- collar with an address tube or tag
- comb and brush
- possibly some cat grass
- cat flap
- some toys

Litter box with cat litter

The litter box is an important part of the outfit. The first box should not be too high, as your kitten will not be able to climb over the edge and will look for a place to do its business that it can easily reach, but which you must keep clean. So don't buy a box thinking your cat will grow into it. Boxes with a lid are also not a good idea. Many cats hate sitting in their own 'air' and in time will stop using the box. Never put the box close to food and drink bowls; your cat will certainly not appreciate that combination. You can use various things as litter. Sand, paper strips and peat dust are suitable. Cat litters that you can buy in shops are generally excellent. Each cat has its own favourite, so in the beginning try different types and find out which one your cat reacts to best. Then avoid suddenly changing brands, as your cat may then avoid the litter box. The box also needs to be cleaned frequently, because a cat will detest a dirty litter box. To disinfect, use household bleach, then rinse with hot water and dry with a paper towel. We might like the scent of a good detergent, but your cat has a totally different opinion!

Travel basket

You will certainly need a travel basket. Even if you've decided never to take your cat on holiday or to have it stay overnight somewhere else, you will need it for visits to the vet. There are many different types of travel baskets on sale. The best are made of plastic and have a door at the top. They are easy to keep clean and to get your cat in and out of. Buy a basket that will be big enough for your cat when it's fully grown.

Scratch pole or plank

A scratch pole or plank may help avoid damage to your curtains or furniture. It is especially a solution for cats that don't go outdoors regularly. Cats scratch to spread their scent for other cats and to keep their nails sharp. This is natural behaviour and you can't train it out of your cat. A scratch pole puts this inevitable behaviour on the right track. Your cat can scratch at its heart's content, but somewhere where it won't damage anything. The scratch pole should be covered with a material with a vertical structure, and should be so high that your cat can stand upright at it. You can get your kitten used to its pole or plank by sprinkling a few drops of valerian on it. Cats find the scent irresistible.

Collar with address tube or tag

Of course, it's possible that your cat may get lost, and anyone that finds it needs to be able to return it to you. A good solution is a collar with a small tube containing your name and address. Choose a collar with elastic. Should your cat become accidentally caught on a branch or other object, the collar should stretch until it comes free, releasing your cat.

There are now also super-light plastic tags for cats, on which your name, address and telephone number can be printed. You can buy these at pet shops.

Brush and comb

A brush and comb are indispensable for daily grooming. Longhaired cats need more frequent grooming than the shorthaired varieties, but you must use a comb with points that are not too sharp and a brush with natural bristles. You can buy these items in a pet shop.

Cat grass

Cat grass is not really necessary for a kitten, because very young animals don't lose hair. They won't ingest hair while cleaning their fur. An adult cat needs this green food to help it vomit fur balls out.

Cat flap

A cat flap is ideal for cats that are allowed outside. Your cat can then get in and out of the house at will and you don't need to leave a window or door open. There are flaps available with an electronic system that will only let your cat in. There are various types of flap available in pet shops.

Toys

A cat is a hunter and its play is a form of hunting, and is a necessary activity. While kittens are still in the nest, they play amongst each other. But a cat without companions definitely needs some toys. These can be a ping-pong ball, a paper ball or special cat toys; it really doesn't matter. Be careful with balls of wool. Cats love playing with these, but they can get entangled in the wool. If you buy special cat toys in a pet shop, make sure parts can't become detached. A cat may swallow these and be suffocated or injured by them.

Cat flap

Toys

Cat grass

Bringing your kitten home

Now you've found that kitten of your dreams and need to set a date with its owner to come and pick it up. A kitten must never be separated from its mother before the age of seven weeks.

Breeders of pedigree cats even prefer an age of twelve to thirteen weeks because of the vaccinations needed. A good rule of thumb for non-pedigree cats is a minimum of eight weeks.

Don't forget to ask the breeder or owner for a feeding plan. It is not a good idea to abruptly change the kitten's food. The first few days in its new home are an enormous change for your kitten. Suddenly, its brothers and sisters are no longer there, and even its mother has gone. Your kitten now needs all the attention it deserves. If you work during the week, try to pick up your kitten as early as possible on a Saturday. You then have the whole weekend to help it get used to its new surroundings, and to spend time with it.

Ask the breeder not to feed the kitten that morning. You're probably going to pick it up by car, and this is almost certainly its first car journey. With a full stomach it may be sick. Take someone with you who can keep the kitten on his or her lap (in a suitable travel basket). Many cats do not like car journeys. If it looks like you're going to make frequent journeys with your cat, get it used to these trips at a young age. If car travel is not really necessary, try to avoid it. Adapt your driving style; don't brake suddenly, take care going round corners and don't accelerate too hard.

Getting to know you...

Once home, carry the kitten indoors in its basket. Then set the basket down on the floor in a closed room (the living room, for example). Open the door of the travel basket and quietly wait for the kitten to come out. Some people still think that a cat should be picked up by the fur on its neck. This was normal in the past, but modern scientific research has shown that this is not correct. The only one that should pick up a kitten by its neck is the mother herself. She does this to bring her young to a safer place. If a human picks it up in this way, it can be painful for the animal. The only correct way to pick up a kitten is as follows: support it with one of your hands under its chest, directly behind the front legs. While you pick it up, support its rear legs with your other hand. Carry it vertically, against your chest. Never pick a kitten up by its forelegs! This can severely damage its still very soft joints.

Stand the travel basket in the room with the door open. It won't take long before the kitten emerges. A young cat is an extremely curious being.

Give the kitten the time to explore its new surroundings, and don't let people rush into the room to cuddle or play with it. In most cases it will miss its mother and nest-mates. Make sure it feels comfortable, don't make too much noise, speak softly and avoid eye contact. Don't pick it up at once and only stroke it if you're sure it likes it. Give it something tasty in the form of a cat snack or a piece

of dried cat food, and let a ping-pong ball roll across the room.

The room is temporarily its new home. Check that everything it needs is there: the litter box, food and drinking bowls (don't put the litter box too close to the food and drinking bowls), its toys and a nice place to sleep. After a while, put the kitten onto its new litter box and then in its basket. It will quickly learn exactly what these mean.

How long this period of assimilation should last is difficult to say. One cat is bolder than another, and the surroundings also play a role. Kittens can be frightened by sounds that are normal for us because we're used to them (radio, television, the parrot). If you frighten your kitten during this period with the noise of the vacuum cleaner or its nozzle suddenly appearing next to it, you're off to a bad start. Try to avoid these sorts of situations.

As we already said, your cat's bed should be dry and away from draughts. However, don't try to force it to sleep in a particular place. It will need a considerable portion of luck to get your cat to sleep exactly there, in that fine basket. After all, cats are very self-willed and like to pick their own place to sleep.

Perhaps you're planning to let your cat outdoors later, but it must first get to feel totally at home before it can leave the house. Keep your cat indoors for about four weeks. It will then be so used to everything that it will find its way back to its own home when it's outside.

Give your kitten a clear name from the beginning. Keep using the name when you're playing with it or cuddling it. It will quickly learn to associate the name with itself. Finally, it will turn its attention to you whenever it hears its name.

Nutrition - feeding your kitten

New-born kittens live from their mother's milk for the first four or five weeks. Then they slowly change to solid food.

They are weaned at eight weeks of age, which means they are completely off their mother's milk. Your kitten is no longer dependent on its mother at the time you take it home.

A healthy meal

Even after you've picked it up, your kitten will continue to develop both mentally and physically.
A good, energy-rich food is very important. Special foods for young cats have high nutritional value. A young cat grows very fast and its body needs plenty of energy to grow properly. As an example: a young kitten needs two to three times as much energy per kilo of body-weight than an adult cat. Fast growth, however, does not mean your cat should get fat, so don't over-feed it. A kitten of eight weeks should be fed five to six times a day, but the amount of food that it gets at each feed is rather small. Some people think their kitten is not getting enough and add a little more, but this is bad for the animal. Stick to the quantity that the manufacturer advises on the packaging. If your kitten has not emptied its bowl within ten minutes, then it's had enough to eat. Take the bowl away and give it a little less, fresh food at the next mealtime.

The word 'healthy' applies to the bowl too. This must be kept properly clean. Good quality bowls of glazed pottery are ideal. Do not add any additives to special kitten food. Should you add calcium, for example, you can

seriously distort the calcium/energy balance in the food. This can affect the development of your kitten's bones. Mixing in fresh meat (heart) is also inadvisable for the same reason. Adding anything to your kitten's food is more likely to cause harm than do any good. Use only ready-made, complete foods. These contain everything your cat needs, even in the later years of its life.

More and more manufacturers pay particular attention to the nutritional needs of cats in different phases of their lives and produce foods formulated especially for each phase.

How often to feed?

From the moment that you bring your kitten home, it should be fed five or six meals per day. At six months, you can switch to three meals per day. Once your cat is a year old, then two meals a day are sufficient (morning and evening).

As we already said, you should stick to the quantities shown on the packaging. But it can happen that you do need to adjust the quantities. Cats that use a lot of energy by running actively outdoors need more energy. On the other hand, cats that only live indoors have a lower energy requirement. But don't forget that

a cat outdoors will catch a mouse now and again, supplementing its energy supply itself.
However, one third of all cats in this country are too fat. A cat that is too fat takes in more energy than it uses. In other words, it eats too much. On a properly fed cat, you should be able to feel the ribs, but not see them. If this is not the case, it is being overfed and you must reduce the size of its meals. But on the other hand, you must always be careful that your cat is getting enough.

Changing foods

Of course, you're free to switch to another sort of food than that which the breeder or previous owner was using. However, do this in steps. Begin by mixing a quarter of the new food with three-quarters of the old. After about a week, make it fifty-fifty, then after a further week three-quarters of the new to one quarter of the old food. The following week you can switch entirely to the new food. Using this method, the transition causes less problems for your kitten.

Not every cat is the same, of course. One will manage fine on a certain food, while another gets constant diarrhoea from it. If this happens, you must stop using that food. Adjust your cat's food until the diarrhoea stops. Your vet will have special foods for this purpose. Then go back to the food your cat was used to, or try something different. Never let diarrhoea go on for more than one day. Young cats, particularly, can quickly become dehydrated. Consult your vet if diarrhoea continues. It is practically impossible for a layman to produce a complete well-balanced diet for a cat, so stick to manufactured foods. These are roughly divided between dry foods and canned food. There is a lot to be said for both types. Canned foods are closest to what a wild cat would eat, namely fresh meat, and most cats are crazy about them.

Moreover, canned food offers the necessary fluids and that is very important. Dry foods are just that -dry- but in terms of composition are just as good as canned foods. They also play a major role in keeping your cat's teeth healthy. The best option is to use both types, so that your cat enjoys the best of both worlds.

Snacks

Of course, you will regularly want to spoil your cat with something special. Don't give it cheese or sausage, as these contain too much salt and fat. For those special moments, there are various products in pet shops that a cat will enjoy, and which are also healthy. There are various aspects concerning the giving of snacks. Firstly, it strengthens the bond between you and your cat. Then the cat will want to play with the snack, reflecting its hunting instincts. A cat will always play with its prey for a while before killing it. This behaviour can easily be observed whenever a cat has caught a mouse. However, it's important to keep an eye on the quantity of snacks you give. Too many 'in-betweens' must be compensated by less food at mealtimes. You can find a wide assortment of healthy snacks in your pet shop or supermarket.

Drinking

A cat must always have fresh drinking water available. Especially cats that are fed a lot of dry food need enough to drink. Practically all cats are crazy about milk, but unfortunately this is not always good for them. Normal milk contains too much lactose, or milk sugar. From the moment that a kitten is weaned, the enzyme that digests milk sugar in its intestines disappears. This is the reason that cow's milk doesn't agree with many cats. Because they can't digest the lactose, they get diarrhoea.

Should you want to spoil your cat with milk once in a while, you can give it special milk for cats. These products have a reduced lactose content, which almost completely eliminates the risk of diarrhoea. Cat milk also contains some special additives, such as higher protein and energy content, extra vitamins and minerals, as well as taurine. This last element is an amino acid that is very important for a cat's health.
It plays an important role in the proper functioning of the heart and eyes. Taurine is also added to cat foods of the better brands.

If you regularly give your cat special cat milk, you must take this into account when determining the amount of food it otherwise gets. The rule is very simple: lots of milk, less food. Cat milk is not a proper substitute for water, so always make sure there's a bowl of fresh drinking water available.

Caring for your kitten

Proper (daily) care is very important for your cat. An animal that is properly cared for runs less risk of becoming ill. Care is not only necessary, but can also be fun. You and your cat give each other your attention, and it's a perfect time for a cuddle.

Grooming

Get your kitten used to a brush and comb session from the beginning. This keeps its skin and coat in good condition and, at the same time, you can check your kitten for parasites (fleas, lice and ticks). You will also have less bother with cat's hairs in the house. There's a big difference between longhaired and shorthaired cats.

Longhaired cats must definitely be brushed every day. Once or twice a week is sufficient for a shorthaired cat. The right equipment is important for grooming. The comb should not be too sharp, and a brush with natural bristles is best. Always comb or brush your pet from head to tail, following the direction the fur lays in. If your cat is bothered by tangles in its fur, remove these as carefully as possible. If you can't comb them out, then carefully clip them away. Reward your cat with a tasty snack after every grooming session. That way, it will soon come to enjoy being cared for.

Eyes

Inspect your cat's eyes every day. Most cats look after their own eyes well by wiping them with their paws, but sometimes you may have to help out if the corners of its eyes get grimy. A piece of sterile gauze or a paper tissue are the best tools here. Cotton wool is less suitable as it can leave fluff behind. Dip the gauze or tissue in lukewarm water (that you've first boiled) and wipe out the dirt from the inside corner of the eye towards the nose.

If your cat regularly has problems with grimy eyes, this could be a sign of an eye infection. In many cases, the mucous membrane around the eye will be reddened and the animal may squeeze its eyes closed in pain. This means a visit to the vet, and usually entails treatment with eye-drops or cream.

Some cats have more problems with their eyes than others. Persians, in particular, are sometimes bothered by watery eyes (tears). This is because their tear ducts easily become blocked because of the special shape of their head. A vet can treat this condition.

Ears

The ears are often forgotten when caring for a cat, but they must be checked regularly. If the shell of the ear is dirty, it must be cleaned. Do this with a clean cotton cloth moistened in warm water or baby oil. Don't use cotton wool because of the fluff it can leave behind. Never penetrate the ear duct with a Q-tip or other object, this will only push any grime further into the ear, and it can even damage the ear. If you neglect caring for your cat's ears, there's a risk of ear infections. A cat that frequently scratches at its ears is probably suffering from dirty ears, an ear infection or ear mites. The latter can be recognised by black grains in the shell of the ear. This discharge looks like coffee grounds or loose earth, and the ear is often injured by the cat's scratching. A visit to the vet's is a must. Remember that ear mites are infectious and you must check any other pets in the house.

Teeth

At first, your kitten will have lovely, sharp white milk teeth. Its final teeth replace these at an age of three to six months.
The change usually passes unnoticed and the kitten usually swallows the milk teeth.
Sometimes, the upper rear teeth don't fall out and remain behind the new teeth. A vet must remove these, otherwise the final teeth may grow in the wrong position.

It's important to get your kitten used to having its teeth cleaned from an early age. Do this with a small brush and some lukewarm water. You can also use a special toothbrush for cats. If you try to get your cat used to having its teeth cleaned later in its life, there's a good chance this will turn out to be a difficult experience for both of you. Cleaning its teeth is important to prevent tartar forming. Neglected cleaning over time will lead to bad breath, a yellow-brown deposit on the teeth (especially on the neck of the teeth) and gum infections. Your cat will eat badly because chewing is painful. If tartar has indeed formed it must be removed under anaesthetic by the vet, so it's best to prevent it by regular tooth care and feeding hard cat chunks at certain times. These also help to prevent formation of tartar to a large extent. There are now even cat snacks available with a particular shape and texture specially developed to clean a cat's teeth and gums.

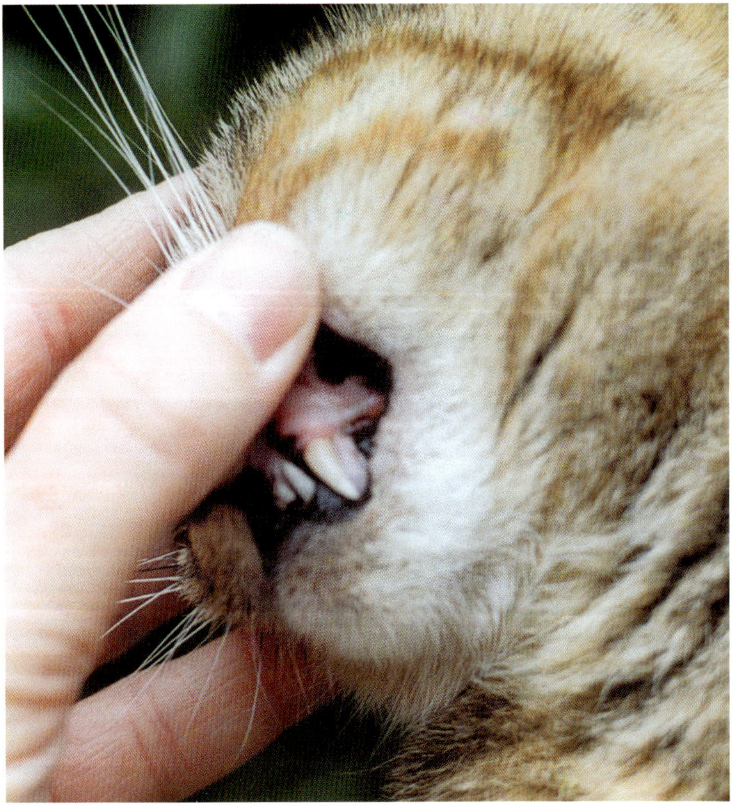

Nails

If there is an animal that pays special attention to its nails itself, then it's the cat. A cat scratches a lot on trees or poles. This keeps its nails at the right length, but it is still important to check your cat's nails regularly. Cats that spend most, or all, of their time indoors can't take care of their own nails properly. Your cat may also be bothered by nails that are too long, so they need to be clipped back. You can do this with a pair of simple nail scissors, but there are also special scissors available in pet shops. Be very careful not to cut into the quick of the nail because this can bleed profusely. If you don't feel sure of yourself, your vet can take care of this task. An indoor cat definitely needs a scratching pole so that it can take care of its own nails as far as possible.

In the bath

In principle, a cat never needs to be bathed. It keeps itself properly clean. It will lick and wash itself a few times a day, but there can be occasions that make a bath necessary. It may have got particularly dirty or need to be treated with a special shampoo (treatment against fleas). Cats don't like being bathed and will do everything they can to avoid it. Hissing, scratching and hitting are all weapons they will happily use to stay dry!

However, if it can't be avoided, use water at approximately 27°C. Make sure the room temperature is not too low and that there are no draughts. Even a cat can catch a cold because a wet coat provides hardly any insulation. If you put your cat in a pillowcase up to its neck, it won't be able to use its nails to scratch you. Dry the animal off with a warm towel and only let it outside when it's completely dry.

One final word about bathing a cat: it's unfortunately not a pleasant task. Hopefully it will seldom be necessary and there are lots of other aspects in your life with your cat that make up for it.

The phases of your kitten's life

A lot of scientific research has been done into the effects that experiences in a young cat's life can have on its behavioural development.

From this we know that a cat's behaviour is influenced to a high degree by positive and negative impulses from its surroundings. If certain experiences are missed, this in itself can lead to behavioural disorders.

Behavioural scientists distinguish between the following phases of a kitten's development into an adult cat.

The vegetative phase

Kittens come into the world completely helpless after a pregnancy of an average of nine weeks. They are deaf, blind and totally dependent on their mother. The first, vegetative phase lasts about two weeks. The kittens do not yet react consciously. They sleep, drink and then discharge the products of their digestion (stool and urine). But they can't yet do this themselves; the mother licks her babies' tummies almost constantly to keep this process going. The kittens find her teats by an inborn instinct, which you can observe up to about the tenth day: the urge to search. They move their heads backwards and forwards, while crawling around in circles. They soon find a part of their mother's body and, a little later, her teats. While drinking, they paw at the area around the teat with their forepaws in rhythmic movements. This 'milking' forms the basis for the later, adult behaviour of tapping on your lap. During this vegetative phase, the kittens are not yet able to keep their own body temperature at the right level, so they lie close

against each other or their mother to sleep. If they lose this body contact and don't find it again at once, they start to miaow loudly.

Kittens can indeed feel and also smell during this period. Subconsciously, they learn to recognise the scent of their litter mates and fellow cats. They can also learn to recognise human scents. If the breeder cuddles each kitten every day, they will learn to recognise humans as their 'fellow cats'.

The transition phase

In the next phase, the hearing and optical nerves now start to develop. The eyes and ears open, on average, between the twelfth and fifteenth day, but the kittens can't yet see and can only distinguish between light and dark. Their eyesight is fully developed by the 21st day. From the sixteenth to eighteenth day, the kittens' sense of smell becomes more conscious; they start to sniff at their brothers, sisters and their mother.

The socialisation phase

Straight after birth, all young animals experience brief learning processes that are intended to help them recognise their own kind, but also other animals. This process is crucial to their survival in the wild where the young first leave the nest around the 21st day.

External influences were insignificant up to now, but now a period of learning begins.

This learning process is equally important for cats that don't live in the wild. It is called socialisation. House-cats must not only be socialised in terms of their own kind, but also towards humans and other pets. They must also get as much exposure to things that will be important to them in later life, such as noises around the house (vacuum cleaner, the stereo system etc.).
A successful socialisation phase is vital for a kitten if it is later to become a fine pet.

Scientific research has shown that kittens will develop into totally shy, wild cats if they don't have contact with humans between the second and seventh week of their life. Practically any attempts to establish a close relationship with a kitten after the seventh week will come to nothing. The only thing to do is to 'tame' the kittens (like wild animals) with plenty of patience. They can indeed overcome their fear of humans, but will never establish a real friendship.

Contact means not only seeing people, but also sniffing at them, cuddling and, especially, playing with them. This must be with men, women and children. If a kitten only has contact with women, it will often later be afraid of men. Imprinting is not only important in terms of humans. A young cat must make acquaintance with other cats, objects, sounds, different situations and other animal varieties. If a kitten has only had contact with humans, and not (or not enough) with other cats, then it can quickly become focussed on humans and won't know how to behave with other cats later. This can even lead to sexual disorders and aggressive behaviour.

Cats that live in the wild learn about everything that they will be confronted with in later life from about the third week on. This means that your kitten should now also be making the acquaintance of all kinds of things that it will be confronted with as an adult cat.

In this period, the young cat learns how to behave towards other living beings. It is by far the most important phase in a cat's life. This is the time the stage is set for the rest of its life. Anything that goes wrong here will be extremely difficult to put right later. Everything that goes well will help to ensure that your cat will be a fine house-mate with good manners towards adults, children and other animals.

On its own feet

Young cats are generally separated from their mother far too early.

Most people think that a six week old kitten is old enough to stand on its own feet. This is not the case, but it will survive changing homes at such a tender young age.

Independence

A kitten needs the proximity of its nest-mates and mother to develop properly. It learns from its nest-mates how to behave later, not only with other cats, but also with humans. Kittens that are separated from their mother too early will later have problems with things such as house-training and adjusting to other cats or humans. So it's best to be patient even though you've set your heart on that pretty little black and white kitten at your neighbour's house. Leave it with its mother for five to six more weeks.

Ideally, cats should only be separated from their mother when they've been fully vaccinated against feline enteritis and cat flu. This can only happen when they're eleven or twelve weeks old. Breeders of pedigree cats usually stick to this time.
If you want to avoid any risk, then leave your new pet where it is until it's fully vaccinated.
If necessary, you can reimburse the previous owner for the costs later.

A room of its own

Cats, and especially those that never go outside, need a place of their own where they can get peace and quiet. This may be a certain room, but also an attic or a cupboard. Cats like to find their own place and will seldom let themselves be driven away from it. If a cat has to share the house with another cat, this need for privacy is even more important. If you want to keep two or more cats, you should really have two or more rooms available. A cat loves to watch the rest of the world from its “own” territory. If two cats have to share the same room (territory), they’re too close for comfort. This might cause the odd skirmish between them. Of course, this doesn’t mean you have to leave the rooms for the cats alone. You carry on living as normal and use their territory at will.

Cats that go outside a lot have less of a need for their own territory in the house. They find their ‘own’ places in the garden. A cat will pick its own area based on the temperature. Cats are true ‘warmth-lovers’. Their ‘place’ will often be close to a source of heat. A window-sill over a radiator or the mantelpiece are favourite spots. There are even hammocks available that you can attach to the central heating. Such ‘aids’ may even help persuade a cat to pick a certain place to sleep.

Bringing up your kitten

Some people believe that a cat can't be trained. Nothing is further from the truth. In contrast to a dog, a cat can't be trained to perform great feats, but it can indeed be taught this or that. They simply have to be made to understand certain behaviour aspects to be able to do things properly later on.

Consistent approach

If you bring a kitten into your home, you need to give a lot of thought beforehand about its upbringing. In other words: what it may do and what not. It's useful to set a few rules together with your house-mates, after which it's important that every member of the family follows the rules rigorously. There's nothing more confusing for a kitten than one person letting it sit on the table and another chasing it away.

If your kitten gets up to something you don't like, you can teach it with a negative stimulus. Imagine your kitten rooting around in your house-plants. At the moment you see it doing this, spray it with water from a plant sprayer, throw a stiff ball of paper at it or drop something nearby that makes a lot of noise (such as a bunch of keys). This will make it jump and stop its wrongdoing. Of course, you're going to have to follow this through for some time before it's completely learned its lesson.

With this method, it's important that the kitten doesn't notice that you are the source of the punishment. Otherwise it will associate the negative stimulus with you, and not with what it was up to. The result will be that it will stop its wrongdoing whenever you're around but will start again as soon as you're out of sight.

House-training

Young cats can quickly become house-trained without any complicated learning process.

In principle, a cat is in itself a particularly clean animal. Females that are very clean themselves often have young that are quickly house-trained. They sometimes drag their young to the litter box when they're still tiny or they demonstrate to their young what they have to do there. This makes life very easy for the owners of such a cat family. They only need to make sure that the litter box is kept clean and the rest takes care of itself. A cat will quickly grasp the significance of the litter box. In fact, it's an extension of their natural behaviour. Outdoors, a cat will also cover its droppings or urine with sand or earth. If you buy a kitten, always ask on what sort of litter it has been house-trained. It may well be that the previous owner used paper shreddings in the litter box. If you then put litter in the box, your kitten won't realise at first that this is the surface it is to do its business on. It will more likely look for a newspaper to sit on. If you want to get it used to a new type of litter, slowly mix more and more of it with the old litter. Then you won't turn a cat that is house-trained into an untrained cat.

If a cat suddenly stops using its litter box, this has nothing to do with its house-training. The box may be dirty or too full, or something else has changed. This could be a different sort of litter or a scent, which the cat doesn't like. There are also cats that don't like to urinate and defecate in the same box. This is quite logical, because cats in the wild don't urinate and defecate at the same spot either. The solution is simply to get a second box. Should your kitten cause an 'accident' however, there is one thing you must certainly not do: rub its nose in its droppings. This is pure cruelty; your cat will only become frightened, and will certainly not have learned a thing. It can also permanently damage its scent organs.

A cat that is unclean may have a medical problem. It could be a sign of a bladder infection. It goes without saying that you should take a cat to the vet's immediately if it suddenly becomes unclean. Only if it's clear that the problem is not a medical one, do you need to think of alternatives. As we said above, it may be that something wrong with the litter box is the problem, but territorial behaviour can also cause uncleanliness. Your vet or pet shop will have products for cats that regularly urinate in the wrong places.

These products are based on the following principle: There are three methods a cat uses to try to mark its territory: spraying, scratching and nuzzling. Whenever a cat nuzzles against something, it wipes the object (for instance a chair leg) with the side

of its head. This gives off aromatic substances (pheromones). These pheromones can be copied chemically. If you apply them to a certain object, the cat will no longer see any point in trying to mark it as part of its territory. Some other cat has already done that. A second way is to try to get the aromatic substances from the cat itself. You can rub some cotton wool along its snout and then stick this with sticky tape to the affected place. An awful form of territorial behaviour is the male's spraying. This leaves a penetrating stink at various places in the house. The best method to combat this is castration. Some eighty percent of male cats react positively and stop spraying.

Anxious behaviour

Cats that didn't come into sufficient contact with humans during the socialisation phase (second to seventh week) are often afraid of people later. It can be very difficult (sometimes even impossible) to form a relationship with such animals. They hide under cupboards, behind beds or in dark corners. They won't even come out to go onto the litter box. Only at night when the house is quiet, will they come out to eat and drink. There is only one way you can try to get such a cat used to you and it requires an awful lot of time and patience. Try feeding your cat by hand to create a bond. Sometimes playing together may help. As long as an anxious cat is

not afraid of other cats, it might help to get a second cat. In this case the anxious cat probably had enough contact with its own kind during the socialisation phase and is not afraid of the other cat. If the other cat is properly socialised towards humans, the frightened cat may slowly get used to humans too.

Car journeys

Cats generally do not like car journeys. That in itself is a good reason to try and avoid them as far as possible, but once in a while a trip in the car will be unavoidable, for instance a visit to the vet or to a holiday kennels. Follow the "teach 'em young" principle. The best way to transport a cat in the car is in a travel basket. Your kitten must get used to its basket. Try the following: open the basket in a favourite place in the house. Young cats are curious and will soon go and explore that 'something new'. In many cases they may even go and sit inside it. Then you set the feeding bowl close by, and a day or two later inside the basket itself. There's no more pleasant way to get your kitten used to something strange.

After a few days, your kitten will be so used to its basket that you can easily put it inside without resistance. Close the basket, put it in the car, and then go for a short trip. Ignore any protests, because if you react to any grumbling or hissing, you're as good as rewarding your kitten for its anxious behaviour and it will certainly do the same thing the next time. Eventually you make the trips somewhat longer so that your cat gradually gets used to travelling in the car.

Kittens and older cats

Cats that are alone a lot will often enjoy having a companion to play with. A second cat is then obviously a good idea. A kitten is the best choice, as an adult cat will accept a young animal more easily than another adult. Older cats are almost always strongly attached to their own territory and there's a high risk of fights for supremacy.
If you take in a kitten, make sure that both animals have enough space. A cat must be able to withdraw to its own spot. If there is a scrap now and again, don't intervene, however much you want to protect the kitten. A hierarchy will only evolve between the cats when one has clearly demonstrated who's the boss. It's exactly this hierarchy that preserves the peace between the animals.

Cat language

Obviously, cats can't speak with one another in words. However, they can make very clear what they want or that something is up. They make use of their voice, but primarily of their body language. They can miaow with their voice, sometimes very loudly, but also very softly. Anyone that has had a cat since it was a kitten knows exactly what a certain form of miaow means. This can range from 'I need attention' to 'I'm hungry', and from 'open the door' to 'come here'. Spitting and snarling are signs of anxiety or aggression. This is accompanied by unmistakable body language; a straight tail, ears laid back and back held high.

Cats can also 'shiver'. They do this mostly when they can see an attractive prey that they can't reach directly.

The most remarkable sound a cat makes is its purring. This is one of the great secrets in a cat's life. A purring cat is usually very satisfied with the current situation; it's on your lap being stroked, or it's nice and warm beside a radiator or in the sun. In a nutshell: purring is a sign of satisfaction. But there are also cases where cats purr when they're in pain. Why this is so is not always clear. Anyone that observes his cat will soon learn to read its body language. A cat in a good mood holds its ears high and forward; a threatening cat has its ears pointed slightly sideways, while a cat in defence holds its ears flat against its head. A cat can also tell us a lot with its tail. A tail held high means a cat approaching you in friendship. If the point of its tail moves backwards and forwards, it's a cat exercising caution. A swishing tail means it's agitated.

Sometimes a cat will suddenly sit washing itself, apparently for no reason. In many cases this is so-called diversionary behaviour. Something has happened that makes it feel not quite itself. It's been up to something it shouldn't, or it just doesn't know what to do with itself. Washing itself serves as a diversionary tactic, as if it's simply saying "You can see I'm not doing anything naughty. I'm just sitting here."

Cats and children

Cats and children are the subject of many a sweet picture, but also of some foolish stories. Many of these stories need never have been told. A cat won't scratch or bite a child just like that, but it will do so to defend itself if it feels threatened. In most cases the cat ends up taking the blame, but often this is actually the fault of humans, the cat's keepers and the parents of the child. It's their job to teach their children how to behave with the animal, and it's also their job to protect their cat against children that are still too young to understand the nature of an animal.

Toddlers and kittens

If you're thinking of taking in a young cat while you also have a baby (or are expecting one), think about what you are about to do! Just like a baby, a kitten needs lots of attention in the first few months. Think about house-training, feeding, playing and up-bringing. After looking after a baby, will you still have the energy left to give a kitten all the attention it needs? Think about the drawbacks too, both of a baby and of a kitten. Imagine you have a baby that cries a lot, costing you precious sleep. How will you react when the kitten has an 'accident' on the carpet just when you were pleased to be able to sit down for a few minutes? A kitten may also be sickly at the beginning and will need extra attention. Do you still have the time and energy to be able to care for it? Whether it's a good idea to get a cat at this time strongly depends on the situation. Someone who is experienced with cats will view it differently to someone who is getting a cat for the first time. And there are also advantages in getting a kitten while there's a baby in the house. By the time the baby is a toddler and starts to crawl, the cat is already used to the child. Cat and child grow up together and are completely adapted to each other. Relating to a cat can also be a valuable contribution to a child's development.

Even when cat and child grow up together, there can still be potentially dangerous situations. Never put the cat in the baby's cot or, better still, in the baby's room at all. A cat won't deliberately hurt a baby but it will use its claws if the child gets too close in the cot and it wants to escape this threatening situation. Once your child starts crawling, new dangers are at hand. A toddler may crawl up behind the cat. The toddler looks on with wide eyes as the cat keeps walking away, but the cat hates it. It withdraws into a corner. The toddler follows it and gets in the corner too. The cat now feels literally 'cornered'. It will start to warn the child by hissing. The baby now finds the cat's noises even more interesting and tries to touch it, at which moment the cat lashes out and scratches the child. This is a dangerous situation, the child's face may have been injured by the cat's claws and an eye injury is a real risk.

Small children are unpredictable and they don't always understand the consequences of their behaviour. A toddler wants to investigate its surroundings. As the toddler approaches, an angry cat will make noises. The toddler doesn't understand that the cat is angry. It finds the situation even more interesting now and will try to do more. Even the most trusted cat will eventually lash out at the young explorer if this goes on too long.

Try to avoid this kind of situation by never leaving young children alone with a cat! If you stick rigorously to this rule, then you can't even go upstairs when the child is

Resting cat

Angry cat

Neutral position

Happy cat

crawling around in the living room and your cat is asleep. Avoid possible conflict situations. Don't let a child and cat hover around you together while you're busy preparing the cat's meal.

Training children

You must explain to children, and thus basically 'train' them, how to keep a cat. They need to learn how to live together with the animal. You must never assume that they know how to handle a cat responsibly just like that.

Teach children

- to respect the cat from the beginning. A kitten is a living being, and not a toy you can do what you want with;
- to handle the cat calmly;
- to learn to understand the cat's language; what is it saying when it hisses or purrs? A child must also learn to recognise when a cat is frightened;
- never to hit or pester a cat; if a cat feels pain, it will bite or scratch;
- how to cuddle the cat;
- to leave the cat in peace when it's asleep or laying somewhere in peace;
- never to run up behind a cat, or to chase a cat;
- to pick up and carry a cat as little as possible. A cat that gets dragged around or held too tight will use its claws and teeth to defend itself. Show your children how to pick up a cat: never by its forepaws.

Misplaced pride

Children are always proud of their newest acquisition. Before you know it, all their friends have been invited to come round and admire their kitten on the first day. However understandable their enthusiasm is, you must temper it. Prepare the child properly for the arrival of its new housemate, and make it clear that the new member of the family is flesh and blood, and is not a cuddly toy. It's vital for the kitten to get the chance to get to know its own family first, so wait a few days with all those visitors.

Children can be wild and agile, and a kitten can easily get frightened. Teach children to behave as calmly as possible with a kitten. Even if patience is not always a strongly developed feature of a child's nature, they must be patient with their kitten. They have to learn that the kitten needs to get used to things too. Hitting and shouting at a cat are out of the question (not only for the children!).

Somewhat older children can help care for a cat. This must be accompanied by an adult, as a child can not take care of bringing up a cat alone. You can add tasks as the child gets older.

Parasites

All cats are vulnerable to various sorts of parasite. These are tiny creatures that live at the expense of another animal.

They feed on blood, skin or other body substances. There are two main types. Internal parasites live within their host animal's body (tapeworm and roundworm) and external parasites live on the animal's exterior, usually in its coat (fleas, lice and ticks), but also in its ears (ear mite).

Fleas

Fleas feed on a cat's blood. They can seriously bother kittens. They cause not only itching and skin problems, but can also carry infections (tapeworm). In large numbers they can cause anaemia and cats can also become allergic to a flea's saliva, which can cause serious skin conditions. So it's important to treat your cat for fleas as effectively as possible, not just on the cat itself but also in its surroundings. There are various medicines to treat the animal itself: drops for the neck and to put in its food, flea collars, long-life foam and flea powders. There are also various sprays available from pet shops that can be used to eradicate fleas in the cat's immediate surroundings.

Choose a spray that kills both adult fleas and their larvae. If your cat travels in your car, you should spray that too, and be sure not to forget its travel basket.

If you own an aquarium, make sure it's properly covered before you spray nearby. These sprays are poisonous for fish and may settle on the water surface, killing your fish.

Fleas can also affect other pets, so you should treat those too. Your vet and pet shop have a wide range of flea treatments and can advise you on the subject.

Ticks

Ticks are small, spider-like parasites. They feed on the blood of the animal or person they've settled on. A tick looks like a tiny, grey coloured leather bag with eight feet. When it has sucked itself full, it can easily be five to ten times its own size and is darker in colour. Cats usually fall victim to ticks in bushes, woods or long grass. Ticks cause not only irritation by their blood-sucking, but can also carry a number of serious diseases. This applies especially to the Mediterranean countries, which can be infested with blood parasites. In our country these diseases are fortunately less common. But Lyme disease, which can also affect humans, has reached our shores. It is important to fight ticks as effectively as possible.

Check your cat regularly, especially when it's been running free in woods and bushes. It can also wear an anti-tick collar. Removing a tick is simple using a tick pincette. Grip the tick with the pincette, as close to the cat's skin as possible, and carefully pull it out. You can also grip the tick between your fingers and, using a turning movement, pull it carefully out. You must disinfect the spot where the tick had been with iodine to prevent infection. Never 'suffocate' the tick in alcohol, ether or oil. In a shock reaction, the tick may discharge the infected contents of its stomach into the cat's skin.

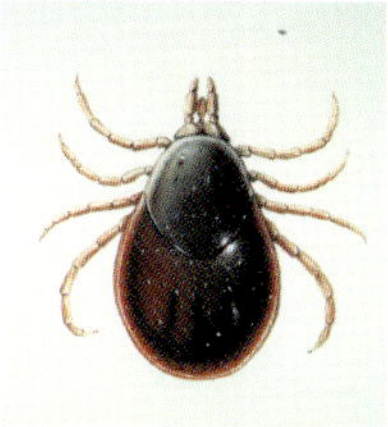

Tick

Worms

Kittens can suffer from various types of worm. The most common are tapeworm and roundworm. Tapeworm causes diarrhoea and poor condition. With a tapeworm infection you can sometimes find small pieces of the worm around the cat's anus or on its bed. In this case, the cat must be wormed. You should also check your cat for fleas, which carry the tapeworm infection.

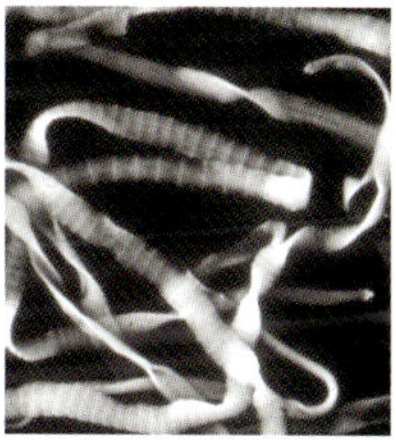

Tapeworm

Roundworm is a condition that reoccurs regularly. Kittens are infected by their mother's milk. Roundworm causes problems such as diarrhoea, loss of weight and stagnated growth. In serious cases the kitten becomes thin, but with a swollen belly. It may vomit and you can then see the worms in its vomit. They are spaghetti-like tendrils. A kitten must also be treated for worms regularly. Older cats that spend a lot of time outdoors and catch mice now and then run a high risk of roundworm infection.

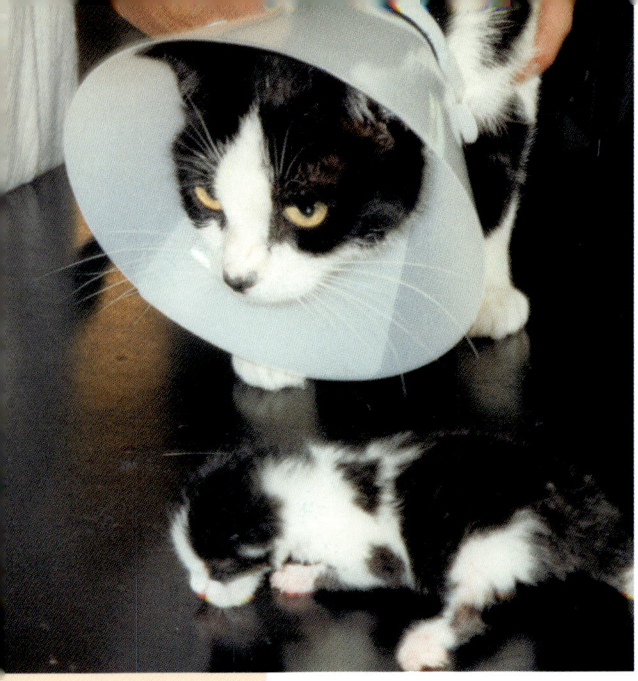

Your kitten's health

Apart from the things you can do in and around your house to make your cat's life safer, proper care is also very important. As we already said, a properly cared for, responsibly fed cat in optimal condition will face much less risk of becoming ill.

The space in this book is too limited to go into the medical to's and fro's of a young cat, but we do want to give some attention to a few important aspects.

Accidents

Cats are playful and adventurous, and this applies especially to kittens. They want to discover the world around them and are sometimes impetuous. However there are a few measures you can take to avoid accidents in and around the house. Don't leave sharp objects lying around, especially with young cats. Think about pins, knives and scissors. Also avoid any contact with strong cleaning agents and painting materials like turpentine.
A less obvious source of poisons are some house plants. Some are especially dangerous (Christmas rose, diefenbachia, oleander, yew, azalea and ivy). The chance of a cat actually eating these is not in itself that high. After all, cats are connoisseurs and won't often take a snack without having sniffed it well. But there is a chance they can get poisoned. This may happen when they've been sitting with their paws on the plant and then lick them.

Open windows and balconies form a much larger risk. You can put in cat gauze to prevent your kitten falling out of the window or from the balcony. In a window the gauze forms a screen, on the balcony it's a fence with a gauze roof. Never forget that a cat is by no means always sure on its feet! It can be seriously injured by a fall. Even if it escapes uninjured, it has almost certainly now got lost and will stray off. Dangers outside the house are more difficult to avoid. The biggest risk is traffic. A cat that's been run over is no uncommon sight. Try as much as possible to keep your cat away from public roads. Males, especially, have the tendency to go off searching for a female in season. If your male has been castrated and is no longer driven by his sexual hormones, this urge to stray will be a little less strong.

Sometimes a cat may fall victim to rat poison, or eat a poisoned mouse. If you can catch it, take it straight to the vet's. Don't forget to take the source of the poison with you if you can. The vet can treat your cat based on this.

Finally, there's a chance your cat may get accidentally locked in a barn or store room. Although you can't avoid this, there is one thing that can help. Make sure it carries a tag, a tube with your name and address, or a chip so that any finder can get your cat back to you.

Diarrhoea

Diarrhoea affects both kittens and adult cats relatively often. Thin droppings point to problems in the intestines. This can have many reasons. It could be an infectious disease, worms, eating the wrong food or a sudden change in its food. Diarrhoea can also be caused by drinking ordinary (cow's) milk. With cats that are often outdoors, it's almost impossible to tell what's wrong. You never know what they may have eaten.

If your cat is suffering from diarrhoea you must not only observe its droppings, but also the total impression it makes. If diarrhoea is accompanied by fever, vomiting or listlessness, then it's time for a visit to the vet's. If your cat has only slight diarrhoea but otherwise appears healthy, give it more easily digestible food. This usually solves the problem. An example of such a food is boiled chicken with rice, or a special diet food that you can get from your vet. It's useful to keep a can or two at home so that you don't need to make a special errand. These foods are suitable for both kittens and adult cats.

When the diarrhoea has passed, revert to your normal food. Whatever you do, don't starve your cat. With some animals, fasting can help bring the intestines back to normal, but cats can not survive without food. They can even suffer from liver conditions if they don't eat for a few days.

Vomiting

It always looks serious when a cat has to vomit. The animal shakes

and looks cramped. But vomiting is usually a part of the grooming process. Cats groom their coats several times a day. They lick and clean themselves and by doing this they ingest loose hairs. These hairs gather in the stomach and finally form so-called hair-balls. These irritate the stomach lining. The result is that they vomit these hair-balls out of their stomach. Cats initiate the vomiting process themselves by eating grass. If your cat never goes outside then it's a good idea to buy a small box of cat grass.

If your cat vomits frequently, then something is wrong. Just like diarrhoea, the reason may be an infectious disease or worms. But it is also possible that it's suffering from a metabolic disorder or poisoning.

A cat that vomits heavily and also displays other symptoms must be taken to the vet's as fast as possible. If your cat appears otherwise healthy you can try to address the problem with a more easily digestible food, but make sure it gets enough food and (especially) that it keeps it down, because fasting is bad for a cat.

Feline Urolithiasis

Feline urolithiasis is a frequent problem, especially with older males. A cat is fully grown at about eight months, so if you've got a young male you could be faced with this condition at some time. Urolithiasis is a condition where tiny crystals cause inflammation in the bladder and urinary tract. This causes severe pain when the cat passes water. A cat with urolithiasis spends a lot of time on the litter box and passes small amounts of urine, sometimes with blood. The worst scenario is that the crystals block the urinary tract and the animal can no longer pass water at all. This needs immediate intervention by a vet. Don't wait hoping it will pass away by itself, because that will not happen! The vet can help by prescribing a course of antibiotics and a special diet.

The precise cause of urolithiasis is not yet known. However, it is known that certain factors play a role. These are obesity, too little exercise and infrequent urination due to the cat not drinking enough. To avoid urolithiasis make sure your cat drinks enough and stays active. Then it won't get too fat and will urinate properly, which rinses the urinary tracts. Once a cat has had urolithiasis it must eat a special diet for the rest of its life.

Vaccination

Fleas, worms and ticks are certainly unpleasant little beasts, but at least one can see them with the naked eye. However cats can also become seriously ill due to invisible 'pests', and vaccination is one of the most important measures you can take to keep your cat healthy. Cats can be vaccinated against a number of serious illnesses. Because the importance of vaccination cannot be over-emphasised, we'll cover a few diseases and their consequences here:

Cat flu is a highly infectious condition of the upper bronchial tracts. It is a condition that quickly gets worse, accompanied by high fever, and usually causes lasting damage. Infection is by direct contact and inhalation.

Distemper *(Feline Panleukopenia)* is an often fatal virus infection that, among other things, affects the digestive tracts. Kittens are especially vulnerable. Annual vaccination is essential to prevent your pet being infected. The disease is passed on in droppings.

Rabies is a virus that affects the nervous system and brain. If not treated in time, this condition can also be fatal for humans. Rabies is passed on by the bite of an infected animal living in the wild. Rabies doesn't exist in the UK

thanks to the animal quarantine laws, however your cat must be vaccinated if you plan to take it abroad. There are strict regulations covering the bringing of animals into the country. Contact your vet well in advance if you are planning to take your cat abroad.

Cat leukaemia is less common than the diseases covered above, but is just as dangerous. It is a virus condition that can lead to the blood cells being attacked and even the formation of tumours. The virus attacks the natural immunity system, leaving the animal unprotected against mould, bacteria and other viruses. These in turn can cause other diseases. Cat leukaemia is spread by direct contact, usually by bite wounds *(saliva)*.

FIP *(Feline Infectious Peritonitis)* is a virus sickness that can appear in two forms. The wet form causes fluid to form in the chest or belly cavity. The dry form causes inflammation in various organs. FIP is spread via droppings.

Chlamydiosis is a bacteria which is active in the development of cat flu. It is spread by direct contact and inhalation.

It is impossible to protect your cat against these diseases without vaccination. Vaccination is nothing other than a way of helping the animal create antibodies. A vaccine is a substance that consists of a certain amount of the virus or the bacteria to be fought. These viruses or bacteria have been processed (weakened) to make them safe. A vaccinated animal had them injected into its body and then creates antibodies. It can then no longer be infected by those viruses or bacteria. Even cats that never go outside should be regularly vaccinated.

The infections can even get into that isolated flat on the tenth floor, on your or your visitors' shoes for instance.

Many vets will send a reminder for the annual vaccinations. They are registered in a special booklet so that you can easily check yourself when the next vaccinations are due.

Vaccination plan

Vaccinations are not mandatory if you keep your cat in and around your house, but if you need to put it into kennels then these will certainly require certain vaccinations. Your cat must also be wormed. Your vet will have a special vaccination plan to give your pet optimal protection. This plan is as follows:

At nine weeks: vaccination against enteritis, FeLv and cat flu.
At twelve weeks: vaccination against enteritis, FeLv, cat flu and possibly rabies, leukaemia. This vaccination must be renewed annually, as the antibodies in the blood slowly degenerate.

Cats that are first vaccinated as adults get a booster injection after four weeks. Then they must also be vaccinated annually.

If you plan to take your cat abroad, it must be vaccinated against rabies. This vaccination is only valid after one month. Get in touch with your vet well in advance if you plan to take your cat abroad or if you plan to put it into kennels.

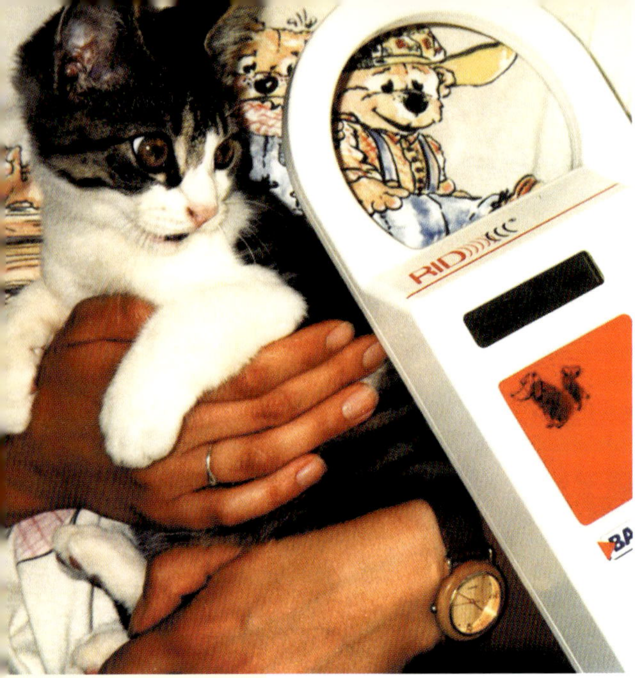

Electronic identification

A modern and effective way to find your cat if it has strayed is the micro-chip. This system is much kinder to the pet than the old method of tattooing.

An ISO chip that is standardised worldwide, and is about the size of a large corn of rice, enables animals to be identified electronically. The vet injects the chip under the skin with a syringe. The procedure is practically painless, and your pet will not be bothered by the chip afterwards.

An electronic identification system consists of the chip (a so-called 'transponder'), a reader device and a database. The chip information is stored on national databases so that any animal can be quickly identified.

The ISO chip has a unique identification code consisting of 15 digits. This code often starts with a country number, so that the country of origin of the animal can be identified (this may be required if you are in another country with your cat). The biggest advantage of electronic identification is that this unique code can not be changed or deleted. The chip consists of a sealed tube of bio-glass containing the microchip and a tiny wire that acts as the antenna. The bio-glass ensures the chip is not rejected but grows together with the tissue. The chip itself does nothing; there are no batteries in it, and its service life is practically unlimited. The reader is a transceiver. It emits a harmless radio signal that activates the chip, which then responds with the cat's identification code. The code appears on the reader device screen.

A chip offers clear advantages over other means of identification. A cat may lose its collar and tag. Tattooing was until recently the usual means of identification, but it is a painful and time-consuming procedure, which usually requires an anaesthetic for adult animals. Tattooed numbers often fade over time or become unreadable under the fur in the ears.

Most pet owners have their pets identified and registered so that they can be returned quickly if they get lost. Thousands of stray or lost animals wind up in animal shelters every year. Cats often never get returned to their owners, after all: all those cats with black and white markings look alike. Most animal ambulances and shelters are now equipped with a reader device. A 'chipped' animal will certainly find its way back home again.

Apart from quickly identifying missing animals, a good identification mark can also be coupled with the documents concerning the animal involved (proof of ownership, health certificate, vaccination booklet, pedigree and insurance number). And finally, effective identification is very important for the buying and selling of pets and for breeding and health programmes.

Tips for your kitten

- Make sure your cat doesn't get too fat. The right amount of food and plenty of exercise (play!) is the golden rule.
- A farm cat will almost always stay shy.
- The male's spraying and the female's season are natural phenomena that (usually) stop after castration.
- A scratch pole will help save your furniture and curtains.
- Give a kitten plenty of time to explore its new environment.
- A kitten is not a toy!
- Don't only fight fleas, but also their eggs. Treat the area directly around your cat's sleeping place!
- A cat only needs to be bathed in exceptional circumstances.
- Keep car journeys with your cat at a minimum. Cats hate travelling in cars.
- Be consistent when teaching your kitten what it may and may not do.
- Try to pick up your kitten from the breeder's early in the morning.
- Start early with brushing and combing so that your kitten quickly gets used to it.
- Never pick a kitten up by its forepaws.
- Two kittens do less damage than one.
- Give your cat a collar tag with your phone number.

Clubs

Becoming a member of a cat fancy club can be very useful for good advice and interesting activities. Contact the GCCF in case addresses or telephone-numbers have changed.

The Governing Council of The Cat Fancy Club Great Britain or GCCF
4 - 6 Penel Orlieu
Bridgwater, Somerset
TA6 3PG, UK
Tel: +44 (0)1278 427575
Email: info@gccfcats.org
http://ourworld.compuserve.com/homepages/gccf_cats/index.htm

GCCF affiliated cat clubs list

Website list clubs:
http://ourworld.compuserve.com/homepages/gccf_cats/clubs.htm

Cat clubs

A directory of cat clubs and societies.
This directory lists some of the many breed societies and area cat clubs in the British Isles.
http://members.aol.com/cattrust/catclubs.htm#s

Cat club Northern Ireland

Catclub.net
8 Deramore Gardens
Belfast, N. Ireland
BT7 3FN
Tel: (028) 90597251
Email: charlotte@catclub.net
http://www.catclub.net/home.cfm

Other books from About Pets

- The Boxer
- The Border Collie
- The Cavalier King Charles Spaniel
- The Cocker Spaniel
- The Dalmatian
- The Dobermann
- The German Shepherd
- The Golden Retriever
- The Jack Russell Terrier
- The Labrador Retriever
- The Puppy
- The Rottweiler
- The Budgerigar
- The Canary
- The Cockatiel
- The Parrot
- The Lovebird
- The Cat
- The Dwarf Hamster
- The Dwarf Rabbit
- The Ferret
- The Gerbil
- The Guinea Pig
- The Hamster
- The Mouse
- The Rabbit
- The Rat
- The Goldfish
- The Tropical Fish
- The Snake

Key features of the series are:

- Most affordable books
- Packed with hands-on information
- Well written by experts
- Easy to understand language
- Full colour original photography
- 70 to 110 photos
- All one needs to know to care well for one's pet
- Trusted authors, veterinary consultants, breed and species expert authorities
- Appropriate for first time pet owners
- Interesting detailed information for pet professionals
- Title range includes books for advanced pet owners and breeders
- Includes useful addresses, veterinary data, breed standards.

about pets

The kitten

Scientific name:	*Felis cattus*
Birth weight:	85-120 grams, depending on the breed
Weaning:	after 7 weeks
Independent:	after 8 weeks
First heat:	5 to 6 months
Age castration, spaying:	male: 8 - 10 months old female: appr. 9 months old